Make your Move Magically Marvelous!

by Gail Van Kleeck

The Home-Decorating Fairy Godmother

*Bringing the Magic of
Possibility into
Your Home and Your Life*

Make Your Move Magically Marvelous! Gail Van Kleeck, 2015, published by Abundant Enterprises

First Edition. Printed and bound in the United States of America.

All rights reserved. No part of this book may be reproduced in any form without permission in writing from the author.

Copyright © 2015 Gail Van Kleeck

ISBN-13: 978-0692576731
ISBN-10: 0692576738

Library of Congress Cataloging
Publication Data November 2015

Van Kleeck, Gail
Make Your Move Magically Marvelous!

Moving

    Make Your Move Magically Marvelous!
    by Gail Van Kleeck

Decorating

    Make Your Move Magically Marvelous
    by Gail Van Kleeck

Table of Contents

Introduction 5
What We Focus On Is What We See 9
Create a Moving Planner 11
Build More Positive Paradigms 21
Sort Your Belongings
   by Category 25
Use Quarter-Inch-Scale
   Floor Plans 35
Consider Your Storage 39
Pack with Unpacking in Mind 43
Prepare For Moving Day 49
Make Your Moving Day Magically
Marvelous 61
Final Thoughts 67
Books and CD's
   by Gail Van Kleeck 73

Introduction

People who are planning a move to different and sometimes smaller surroundings are often overwhelmed by the thought.

They don't know what they will do with the things they've accumulated. They dread the chore of weeding out their belongings. They feel sad about leaving their existing home and are generally confused and anxious because they don't know where to start.

There is an emotional as well as a physical component of moving, but the emotional component is all too frequently ignored.

While I promise to give you countless simple-to-implement suggestions for making the physical part of your move easier, focusing first on the emotional part will make it a more positive and less overwhelming experience.

Before I begin, however, I'd like to tell you a short story about a couple who took their two young children on a camping vacation.

The four of them were riding their bikes along a path in the woods when they came upon a sign that read "Naturalist Center." Just as the father was thinking how nice it would be for his children to see examples of plants and animals indigenous to the area, three completely naked bikers pedaled past them.

"How am I going to explain that to my children?" he wondered. Then his thoughts were interrupted by his oldest son. "Hey Dad, did you see that?" the six year old shouted. "They weren't wearing their helmets."

I love this story because it's clean and funny and also because it so perfectly illustrates that what we focus on is what we see.

What We Focus On Is What We See

Despite what many of us may believe, it has been scientifically proven that our brain can only truly focus on one thing at a time. This means every moment we spend thinking thoughts that cause us to feel anxious or fearful is a moment in which we are unable to see and embrace more positive and empowering possibilities.

A paradigm is something we have always believed to be true and nearly all moving-paradigms contain the belief that it will be overwhelming and stressful.

This is often because most people who are moving don't know where to begin, so they focus first on the difficulties they associate with moving. This makes it nearly impossible for them to imagine the freedom, flexibility and limitless possibilities of a new home. It also increases their level of stress and reinforces the negative message of most moving-paradigms.

Beginning your move by creating a vision of your new home will make every moving decision easier.

Create a Moving Planner

There are so many little details involved with a move and gathering them together in an easily accessible place is much better than trying to keep everything in your head, or worrying that you have forgotten something important.

Begin by buying a good quality notebook to use as your Moving Planner. Put your calendar, contact information, thoughts and miscellaneous notes related to your move in the BACK of your planner. It will be easier to organize those thoughts and notes if you use separate pages for each of your new home's rooms.

Use the FRONT PAGES of the Moving Planner to write your vision for your new home.

It is important to do the suggested writing in this chapter.

It won't take long and your responses can give you insights that will empower you to make your moving decisions with greater confidence.

Don't write about how you would like your new home to LOOK.

Write instead about how you would like to USE IT, how you would like it to FEEL and how it can SUPPORT and ENHANCE YOUR QUALITY OF LIFE.

Be as creative and outrageous as you've ever dared be. Don't limit yourself with worries about your budget. Imagine you are drawing a beautiful outline of your completed new home so you can fill in the details later, then dream the fullest and richest dream you can imagine.

When I moved to my home, more than thirty years ago, I had just come to the end of a long-term marriage and was starting life anew. I was frightened and sad and anxious about nearly everything. This is the new home vision I wrote for myself back then. I am sharing it with you now in the hope it will inspire you to write a new home vision of your own.

I want my home to feel safe and peaceful and healing. I need my little cottage to be my haven. I need it to be a place where I can be comfortable, where I can go barefoot, where I can sit by the fire or read a book. I want my home to be a part of nature. I need it to have a garden and a yard.

I would like it to be pretty, not necessarily beautiful. I need it to welcome my friends and make them feel comfortable and accepted. I want places in every room for genuine conversation. I need places for the simple things I treasure: my books, that awkward piece of pottery my son made his first year in camp, my grandmother's tea set and the paper-mache' angel with pendulous breasts my sister sculpted for me one Christmas.

I want it to be a simple, straightforward, honest and gentle place. I need a kitchen with room enough to encourage those who would like to help. I need a well-stocked pantry to enhance my home's feeling of abundance.

I need my home to be a place where people can dance in the kitchen or sing around the piano, a place where they can share their feelings honestly, where they never need to pretend, a place they look forward to returning to and reluctant to leave.

Leave a few blank pages after you think you've finished writing your new home vision so, if you wish, you can add to it later on. Then expand and enrich your vision by thinking about your responses to the following questions:

- Think about the person you were when you moved into your current home. What, beyond the wrinkles or occasional aches and pains, has changed for you since then?
- How have those changes affected who you are and what you need from your new home?
- What was important to you when you moved into your current home and what is important to you now?

- What would you like to do in your new home that you haven't had the time, the energy or the desire to do until now?

Through my many years as a designer I have helped countless people move into surroundings that were new to them.

Then, just as I was writing **Make Your Move Magically Marvelous**, I made the decision to move myself... this time to somewhat smaller surroundings.

That decision affected the content of this book and inspired me to share what I have learned through personal experience as well as through the experiences of the countless clients I have worked with throughout the years.

It also meant that I needed to write an entirely different vision for my new home before I began making my moving decisions. I also needed to answer the same questions I have asked you.

Taking time to do that helped me leave the home I had loved for so long and gave me the courage to look forward with optimism and faith.

P.S. I am a very different person now than I was thirty years ago, when I wrote my first new home vision. I am more confident, I laugh lots more and I have found someone to love who also loves me.

The adjectives I used to describe how I wanted my home to feel in that more tumultuous and tender time of my life were words such as safe, haven-like, welcoming and peaceful.

Now, while I want my new home to feel that way too, I would also like it to feel happy, alive and filled with possibility.

As I was making my recent move, I did something I had never asked a client to do. I used the CENTER part of my Moving Planner for jotting down quick daily notes about some of the things that were contributing to my move.

The results were worth the effort. My moving notes helped me stay focused on what I had already accomplished and kept me from using my time and energy worrying about what I still needed to do.

Since it made such a difference for me, I am sharing some of my daily observations with you in the hope they will inspire you to create a moving journal of your own.

February 13: *The goal for selling our home is to make it look as though its new family could see themselves* moving into it without making any major changes. Paul, the home improvement contractor, started work today. He is going to paint all the walls and ceilings and I am going to paint the woodwork. All is well. All is well.

February 15: Paul had a conversation with me about painting the woodwork. He says he has seen the level of my painting expertise and doesn't want my workmanship to diminish the quality of his. We have negotiated a price for HIM to paint woodwork. Honestly, when I think of how much of it there is, I'm relieved. All is well. All is well.

March 18: We are getting closer and closer to the time we will be moving. I have been drawing floor plans for the furniture placement in our new home so we will have a clearer sense of what needs to be replaced and what we will be bringing with us. The Vietnam Vets *came today and picked up twelve bags of things we don't really need. Parker wants to keep our hideous, but very comfortable living room sofa. Otherwise we are great. There is so much to think about. All is well. All is well.*

April 12: *We are replacing our old sofa with a beautiful blue-gray sectional. Parker is alright with that because we are also getting a larger TV. All is well. All is well.*

Build More Positive Paradigms

There are countless paradigms related to the physical part of moving and all of them are worth questioning. While they may contain an element of truth, that truth is often based on our focus and on the way we choose to see and experience our move.

One of the paradigms you may have heard and believed is that before you can move you need to GET RID OF as many of your belongings as you can.

What if you could create a more empowering paradigm? What if you didn't focus on what you need to GET RID OF?

What if you focused instead on KEEPING only the things that hold precious memories, make you happy or are truly necessary and useful?

Think for a moment about the power of words and phrases and how they affect your beliefs and actions. Phrases such as "throwing out" or "getting rid of" can make you feel anxious or even defensive about clinging so tightly to material things.

What if you changed that "getting rid of" paradigm by thinking of yourself as a generous person who wants more freedom, less responsibility, fewer things to weigh you down and who also welcomes the possibility of living a simpler, less cluttered and more peaceful life?

Remembering that a paradigm is something we have always believed to be true, there is also a paradigm about the best way to sort your belongings before you move, which you may also wish to question.

That paradigm is the belief that you need to prepare for your move by going through your belongings one room or one closet at a time. What if that paradigm isn't true?

What if it's easier and more efficient to sort through your belongings by category?

Imagine that one of your categories is pencils. If you go through your pencils one room or one drawer at a time, you are likely to pack more pencils than you need because you have no idea of how many pencils you actually have.

Now imagine going through your desk drawer, your purse, the junk drawer in your kitchen, the cabinet beside the telephone, the table beside your favorite chair and collecting all the pencils you can find.

Then imagine putting them on your kitchen table and sorting through all of them at once.

When you see all of your pencils together you will be less likely to worry about having enough and more likely to choose only the ones you will actually need in your new home.

Although pencils are fairly small items, they are a symbol of all your other belongings.

Gathering your belongings into categories and choosing only what you love and need, can empower you to live a simpler, less cluttered and more peaceful feeling life.

Sort Your Belongings by Category

Although it's possible to start your sorting with any category, I suggest that you focus on your artwork first.

This will give you an immediate sense of how it feels to sort your belongings by category … Once you get started, you'll be surprised to discover how good it feels.

Walk through every room in your home, stop in front of every piece of artwork on your walls and ask yourself just one question: **"IS THIS SOMETHING I WANT TO WAKE UP TO AND ENJOY EVERY DAY FOR THE REST OF MY LIFE?"**

If your answer is "YES" put a sticker or post-it on it and move along to the other artwork throughout your home.

The pieces you choose to bring with you when you move are likely to have several important things in common:

- You loved them the moment you saw them and have a story to tell about them.
- They either hold memories of people who are precious to you or remind you of places you have visited or would still like to see.
- Their total function in your life is simply to make you smile.

The pieces of artwork you can let go of with relative ease are also likely to have several other things in common:

- They were given to you as a gift and you hung them because

you didn't want to seem unappreciative or make the person who gave them to you feel badly.
- You had an empty wall to fill and bought a pleasing piece of artwork to fill it.
- They are something you liked at one time, but have outgrown.
- They don't really reflect the way you would like your new home to feel.

After you have made a decision about the artwork on your walls, go through your attic and basement and ask yourself if any of the artwork you have stored there is something you want to wake up and enjoy for the rest of your life.

Once you have chosen what you feel happy about bringing with you, put the other artwork together in one place and invite your family and friends to take what they would like.

Then remembering your intention to be generous, make a pick-up appointment with your charity of choice, silently thank the remaining pieces for their service and wholeheartedly give them away.

The good news about sorting through your belongings by category is that it will empower you to take fewer belongings with you when you move.

The bad news about this kind of sorting is that it can disrupt or create disorder in nearly every room of your home…. but there is good news in that bad news.

What I discovered as I did this myself, was the more disorder I temporarily created, the less I grieved about leaving the home I loved.

The next sorting category is books. Begin by collecting boxes for your books. Liquor boxes are especially good, because they are sturdy and small enough to lift when they are full.

You will also need a good supply of paper bags with handles for carrying the books you don't want out to your car, so you can take them to a library or to the charity of your choice.

Choose the room in your home that contains most of your books and put up a card table there so you can bring all the books in your home into just that one room. Sort your books into categories based on their content and ask yourself these three questions:

- Is this a book I once loved and would like to re-read?
- Is this a book I would like to loan or give to a friend?
- Will I use this as a reference book, or do I now prefer to do

my research electronically?

Then put the books you've decided to keep in boxes and label each box with the category of its contents and the place you would like those contents to be placed. Put the books you've decided not to keep in paper bags and carry them out to your car.

If you are planning to bring one or more of your bookcases to your new home, there are four simple steps that will make unpacking your books much easier.

- Arrange your books by category and put them in your bookcase.
- Label each shelf with a different number.
- Take a photo of your bookcase, so you can refer to it when you move.

- Then put each category of books into a box and label the box with its contents category, its shelf number and the room in which your bookcase will be placed.

Once you have sorted your artwork and books, focus on your accessories and then move on to the different categories in your kitchen and your clothing.

Every major category, such as accessories, can be sorted into smaller sub-categories.

If you are sorting your accessories, the sub-categories could include: statues or figurines, vases, candle sticks, decorative pottery, decorative glass pieces, bookends or paper weights.

If one of your main kitchen categories is dishes, your sub-categories might include mixing bowls, salad bowls, serving dishes, casserole dishes.

If you are sorting clothing, your sub-categories could be: hats, hand bags, shoes, boots, blouses, cardigan sweaters, pull-over sweaters and turtle neck sweaters.

Some of these sub categories have sub-categories of their own. Shoes, for example, might have sub-categories such as sneakers, sandals, dress shoes, black shoes, red shoes, winter shoes and boots, some of which may have several sub-categories of their own, such as: snow boots, dress boots, work boots, tall boots and shorter boots.

Being as specific as you can be about the categories you are sorting has many VERY IMPORTANT BENEFITS.

- You will reassure yourself that you have enough.

- Your new home will be easier to care for because it will contain only the things you really love and need.
- It will be easier not to keep saving the "stuff of life" you've been saving for years...just in case you might need it someday.
- It will make unpacking much easier.
- Since unpacking will be easier, you will immediately feel happier and more "at home" in your new surroundings.

34

Use Quarter-Inch-Scale Floor Plans

Deciding which pieces of your current furniture will serve you the best is an important part of creating a vision for your new home.

While you can measure the walls in your new home as well as the furniture you would like to bring with you, it's difficult to imagine how the individual pieces will work together, without using a quarter-inch-scale floor plan.

If you already have an architectural plan for your home all you need is quarter-inch furniture templates.

If you have been given a floor plan that fits nicely on a regular eight and a half by eleven sheet of paper, chances are it is NOT quarter-inch scale.

If you need guidance in creating a color palette, arranging your artwork and accessories, choosing new furniture and window treatments, combining patterns or making your home uniquely your own, you will also find those topics in my decorating guide.

If you don't have quarter-inch-scale floor plans you can copy the furniture templates and learn to draw your own floorplan by reading the easy-to-implement directions in my interior design e-book, *The Magical Interior Design Guide*, by going to www.homedecoratingfairygodmother.com

It is almost impossible to overstate the value of using quarter-inch-scale floor plans.

A floor plan can show you whether your current eighty-four inch sofa will fit in your new family room, or if a sectional or smaller seating piece would create a better conversation area.

It can guide you in creating better storage and placing your overhead lighting. It will show you the best area rug sizes to use in your rooms. It will help you use what you already own. It will increase your sense of possibility, so your completed home will better serve your needs and make you want to hug yourself every time you walk through its door.

Consider Your Storage

No matter how beautifully your rooms are arranged or how comfortable and inviting they feel, if they don't have adequate storage they won't fully serve your needs.

Very few homes have enough well-planned storage. If you are moving into smaller surroundings, the amount of storage you create can directly affect your long-term happiness.

Because storage is so important, my decorating book, **The Magical Interior Design Guide,** devotes an entire chapter to room-by-room-storage. The following suggestions, which are not in my book, are possibilities you may also wish to consider.

If one of your rooms has a wall without a window, you can build-in or buy enough twenty four inch deep cabinets, or bookcases with doors, to cover as much of your windowless wall as possible.

Make sure what you choose has adjustable shelving and buy several additional shelves. Measure the length and width of one of the shelves, then go to a store that has a good selection of plastic containers.

Look for storage containers that are just a little shorter and a little narrower than the shelves, so they will slide in and out as though they were drawers. The optimal height of these containers/drawers is from seven to ten inches, depending on what you plan to store.

You can use containers as drawers in your kitchen's base cabinets or in almost any other storage piece that has shelving behind its doors. Storing your belongings in drawers is more efficient than stacking them on shelves because drawers allow you to use all of your available space, while stacked items usually leave an unused space above them.

If your space is limited, look for vertical storage such as tall furniture, bookcases and narrow armoires or cabinets. Consider using a decorative shelf in one of your rooms, so you can display the belongings you love without cluttering your table tops.

Repurpose your existing furniture. Think about using a long bedroom bureau as a console on which to place your family room TV. Consider using the decorative chest you already own as a hamper or use the lower drawer of a dresser instead.

My former mother-in law declined our offer to live with us for a while because she said she couldn't possibly live in a home with such poor housekeeping.

In truth, our home was always reasonably clean, but it was also sometimes cluttered. While at the time, I was offended by her statement, I took it to heart and began looking for ways to create better storage. This is what I found:

If there is a place in every room for everything that needs to be stored and used in that room, there is always the possibility, that sooner or later, those things will be put away.

Pack with Unpacking in Mind

Correctly labeled boxes can make a HUGE and DRAMATIC DIFFERENCE in the ease with which you complete your move.

BEFORE YOU OR YOUR MOVERS TAPE YOUR BOXES SHUT, BE SURE EACH BOX IS LABELED ON ALL FOUR SIDES AS WELL AS THE TOP.

It is often necessary for movers to pile boxes on top of one another. If your labels are on the sides of your boxes as well as the top, you will be able to find the ones you need more easily.

If each of your labels contain the following specific information, you will substantially simplify your unpacking.

- The contents of the box

- The room and the place in that room from which the contents were taken
- The room and the place in that room you would like the box's contents to be unpacked.

If you would like the scarves from the middle drawer in the Master Bedroom dresser to be hung on the hooks on the back of your new Master bedroom closet door, your label needs to look like this: Scarves/ From: Master Bedroom dresser/ middle drawer….To: Master Bedroom/hooks on back of closet door

EVERY MINUTE YOU SPEND LABELING YOUR BOXES WITH THIS SPECIFIC INFORMATION WILL SAVE YOU HOURS OF HEADACHES LATER ON.

This is especially important when you are unpacking and putting away the contents of a kitchen.

While the following suggestions may seem like extra work, you will thank me for them when you are unpacking.

Kitchen Drawers and Cabinets

Before you begin sorting the contents of your existing kitchen, ask permission to go into your new home to take measurements and photographs.

- Bring a measuring tape, a pen, a package of post-it's, a camera or a cell phone with a camera and your Moving Planner.
- Put a post-it on each of your new kitchen's cabinets and drawers.
- Write a different letter of the alphabet on each of the post-its.

- Take measurements of each space.
- Take a photo of each space.

Put this information in your Moving Planner

If that isn't possible, put them in an envelope or small plastic bag so you can put them back up prior to your move. If one of your kitchen categories is casserole dishes, the label on their box will look like this:

Kitchen/Casserole dishes/ From: lower cabinet beside dishwasher/To: Cabinet A.

While you may want to rearrange some parts of your kitchen later, using specific category information on your labels will assure that your kitchen will be basically organized, rather than being arbitrarily unpacked.

Your New Home's Other Storage Spaces.

Once you've completed labeling your kitchen drawers and cabinets, walk through the other rooms in your home and look for closets, cabinets, shelving and any other place that could be used for storage.

Take measurements and photos of each of these places and the room or space in which they are located, then write that information in your Moving Planner. For example: you might describe a space as third floor hall/linen closet.

If your boxes are labeled with this kind of specific information, their contents can be put away sooner and more easily.

The sooner your belongings are put away, the sooner you'll begin enjoying your new surroundings.

There is another huge benefit of paying attention to and measuring all of your new home's potential storage places.

Having a clearer sense of how much storage space you actually have, will empower you to make better decisions about which belongings you choose to bring with you.

Prepare For Moving Day

Two Weeks Before Your Move

The two weeks before moving day are especially important, because the actions you take in those two weeks can affect the ease with which you move as well as how quickly you will feel at home.

The following four suggestions will empower you to move into your new home with a more confident and possibility filled spirit:

- Designate one of your lesser-used, main-floor rooms as your home's temporary box storage area.
- Ask for help and assign clear and specific tasks.
- Gather your moving-tools together.

- Simplify and mail your change of address notifications.

Designating one of your lesser-used, main-floor rooms as a temporary box-storage area is important because, being surrounded by unpacked or partially unpacked boxes in every room will keep you from appreciating and enjoying your new home.

Your temporary box-storage area will be used for boxes that NEED IMMEDIATE UNPACKING. This includes boxes filled with artwork, lamps, lampshades, large accessories and artificial flowers or plants.

These items are typically packed in larger boxes, which take up more physical space. Unpacking them, flattening them and getting them out of your new home as soon as possible will substantially reduce the disorder and confusion of your move.

Your temporary box-storage area will also be used for the boxes that CAN WAIT TO BE UNPACKED. The contents of these boxes may include decorative accessories, books, photo albums and home-office supplies.

Once you've settled into your space, you can take one box at a time from your temporary box-storage area and unpack its contents more leisurely.

Ask five friends or family members to be a part of your moving- team and be specific about what you need from them. This will give them opportunity to participate in the courageous transition you are undertaking and the fulfilling feeling of helping someone they care about.

The Members of Your Moving Team:

The Personal Unpacker (one person)

This person is responsible for opening your wardrobe boxes, putting their contents away and flattening the empty boxes.

You can also ask them to open and put away the contents of boxes containing shoes, handbags, gloves, scarves and other clothing that is typically folded rather than hung.

The Personal Unpacker is usually responsible for unpacking and putting away the towels, toiletries and linens and for making the bed.

The Kitchen Unpackers (two people)

These team members are responsible for unpacking your kitchen boxes and putting their contents away.

The alphabetical letters you put on the contents of your kitchen category boxes, and the corresponding letters you taped to your new home's kitchen cabinets and drawers, will make it easier for your Kitchen Unpackers to set up your kitchen in the way you would like to use it. Once they have unpacked the boxes they need to flatten them and take them out of the kitchen.

The Hostess-with-the-Mostest (one person)

This is the person responsible for providing food and "music-to-work-by" to the movers and your team. She is also responsible for collecting the boxes other team members have flattened and putting them outside your home, or in the place you have previously designated.

Give your Hostess-with-the-Mostest enough money to purchase an assortment of pre-made salads or cold-cuts, beverages, and paper goods as well as fruit, brownies or other easy-to-eat sweets.

Moving day can be physically challenging work for both your team and the movers. If there is a pot of soup simmering on the stove and the evidence of someone providing food, the movers and your moving team will be more likely to stay in your home and maintain their momentum.

The Big-Box Director (1 person)

The Big-Box Director is the person assigned to the temporary box-storage room. This person is responsible for opening and unpacking the big boxes, which usually contain artwork, mirrors, lamps, lamp-shades, larger accessories and artificial plants etc., and then gathering their contents together in that room.

The Big-Box Director is also responsible for flattening the emptied boxes and for guiding the movers in stacking the categories of boxes that do not need immediate packing.

The contents of these boxes may include, small accessories, photo albums, desk or office supplies and other items that do not need immediate unpacking.

One of the secrets of settling comfortably into your new home is to get rid of as many boxes as you can, as quickly as you can.

Because you are familiar with nearly every aspect of your move, assign yourself the title of **Moving Director.**

As the Moving Director, you are responsible for making a copy of each room's floor plan as well as an overall plan for each floor in your new home.

You also need to make copies of the job titles and responsibilities for each team member so you will have time before your move to respond to their questions and concerns.

Gather together the following supplies:

- Masking tape
- Several pens and felt tip markers
- Scissors
- Your Moving Planner
- A box cutter for yourself and one for each of your team members
- And don't forget enough toilet paper for each bathroom, several rolls of paper towels and a spray bottle of Windex or the cleaner of your choice.

You will also need a bouquet of fresh flowers, a candle, some matches and

something festive to eat or drink after the movers leave.

You and your team will be weary, but happy, at the end of the day and you will be glad you thought of doing something simple, yet thoughtful, for them.

One Week Before Your Move

Whether you are moving across the country or just across town, you need to notify your friends, family, and the business and organizations who serve you about your change of address.

Happily, the U.S. Post Office will forward your mail, so you don't need to create additional stress by attempting to send all of these notifications at once.

Happily too, the post office flags the letters they forward to you with a YELLOW STICKER. This means you will be reminded who you still need to notify.

As with your other sorting, it will be easier if you sort your moving notification announcements by category.

The following alphabetized categories will help you:

- Animal Care Givers
- Banks and Financial Service Providers
- Household Services
- Close Friends and Family Members
- Clubs and Organizations
- Credit Card Services
- Health Related Organizations and Doctors
- Household Services
- Government Agencies
- Magazines and Newspapers
- Utilities

Put these categories in your moving planner and leave enough space between them to enter the contact information for the individuals, businesses or organizations associated with that category.

The Night Before You Move

Put the bed linens and pillows for the beds that will be slept in the following night into a plastic bag and put your medications, and personal care supplies into a box or small suitcase so you can put them in your car in the morning. This will help your Personal Unpacker to find and take care of them for you.

Then try to get a good night's sleep. If thoughts about the things you need to do are still going around in your mind, change your focus by going through the alphabet and thinking about something or someone, related to your move, for which you are grateful.

The night before my recent move I did this myself. It was amazing how peaceful it made me feel. Before I reached the letter M, I'd fallen fast asleep. The following things on my list may help you get started:

- I am grateful that this move is ALMOST over.
- I am grateful for my BODY and for the way it let me do almost everything I thought was necessary.
- I am grateful for the COMPASSIONATE and CARING people who have helped me.
- I am grateful for the DREAM I created for my new home and how focusing on it made my move easier.

Make Your Moving Day Magically Marvelous

Start your day by eating something substantial. Just a cup of coffee isn't enough.

Put your bag of linens and the suitcase you packed last night in your car and give your Personal Unpacker your key.

Go to your new home at least an hour before your movers are scheduled to arrive. If you can't go yourself, give someone on your team this to-do list and ask them to be there for you.

Bring your moving tools, the after-the-move celebration items, copies of each room's floor plan as well as your floor-by-floor plans.

Tape a copy of each room's floor plan to a WINDOW in that room, so your movers can put the furniture where you want it.

Tape copies of the floorplans for each floor NEAR THE FRONT DOOR where you and the movers can see them.

This will make it easier for you to show them where to take your furniture and belongings.

The movers are likely to bring your area rugs in first, so they can place the furniture on top of them.

If you use a few pieces of masking tape to mark the place on the floor where you would like the rug to be placed, your move will be easier and the movers will be grateful.

If you want your bed or furniture in a specific place, put a piece of masking tape on the wall to show the movers where you would like them to place the center of that furniture.

Then go into the kitchen and tape the correct letter of the alphabet to each of your cabinet doors and drawers.

Once you've completed those tasks, walk to the front door with a confident smile, knowing you have done everything you could to make your moving day as positive and easy as possible.

Don't make it necessary for people to search for you. Plan to stand at the front door until the movers become familiar with the layout of your home and your moving team is comfortably unpacking.

As the Moving Director you will be responsible for answering questions and for guiding the movers to specific rooms.

This means you will need to be aware of the contents of the boxes they are bringing in, so you can divert the big boxes and the boxes containing photo albums, books and small accessories to the room set aside as the temporary storage area.

It is also your responsibility to help your Kitchen Unpackers by giving the movers specific directions regarding the kitchen category boxes.

Ask them to place the kitchen-category boxes against the wall in a part of the kitchen that doesn't contain cabinets or counters, such as the area set aside for a breakfast table.

If there is no area like that in your kitchen, ask them to pile the kitchen related boxes along a wall just OUTSIDE the kitchen door.

This will give your kitchen-unpacking team more room to move around and will substantially decrease the time in which they can complete their unpacking.

Once the movers and your moving team are comfortable with their tasks, you can relax a little and become more of a hostess, whose job is to make everyone's job go smoothly.

This means you will help out a little now and then, encourage the movers and your team to eat and to take occasional breaks.

Your appreciation and the way you express that appreciation is one of the most important parts of your Moving Director job.

ANOTHER PART OF THE MOVING DIRECTOR'S JOB IS TO FOCUS ON YOUR GRATITUDE FOR WHAT HAS ALREADY BEEN DONE.

The more things for which you are grateful, the more relaxed you will feel… and feeling grateful and relaxed will make an enormous difference in your entire moving day.

After the movers have left, bring out the flowers and light the candle you brought with you, then invite your team to join you in having a glass of champagne or whatever refreshment you have brought to thank them.

There is a certain blessing about being surrounded with the people who have helped you make this incredible journey to a new home. It will be a very long time until you can close your eyes at night without thinking lovingly and gratefully of them.

Final Thoughts

It was surprising to me how quickly I felt at home in my new surroundings. I had expected to miss my back yard and my garden and the always-friendly view of the neighborhood from my kitchen window...but I didn't.

I thought instead of how much I liked the colors in my new home and the way the new furniture I'd purchased blended with the things I have treasured for so long. I also thought about how much I was looking forward to living a simpler life and of all the unknown possibilities that lay ahead.

I didn't drive past my old home for several weeks, as though seeing it might break my heart ... but it didn't.

There is a part of me that feels incredibly disloyal, but there is another part me that feels completely peaceful, happy and contented in my new surroundings.

I wish you great happiness and a rich and fulfilling life in your new home. The most important and precious memories from your past will continue to sustain you…. But now it is time to notice and embrace the possibilities that await you, behind your new front door.

The Author

Gail Van Kleeck loves life. She is an often funny, sometimes wise and insightful woman whose peaceful presence makes her a trusted friend and an empathetic listener.

Her writing contains the persistent, loyal, compassionate and wanting-to-make-a-difference values she learned as a child. It is also a reflection of her seven years as a Hospice volunteer and the way that experience touched and changed her perspective, her relationships, her writing and her nearly forty years as an interior designer.

Gail has written two books related to creating a comfortable, welcoming home, two inspirational/motivational books and one book for children and for the child in each of us.

I Have a Story Teller in My Closet, is the first book in this series of children-of-all-ages books about our perception and what we value. Other books in this series will be available soon.

While she loves both writing and interior design, the most precious parts of her life are her children and grandchildren and the relationships she has with her family of origin as well as with her extended family of choice. She and her long-term life partner, Parker Babbidge, a jazz musician and wooden sailboat builder, live with their Golden Doodle Katie, in Northbridge, Massachusetts.

Gail wishes you and those you love a life filled with countless reasons for feeling grateful.

Books and CD's by Gail Van Kleeck

**Make Gift Giving Easy
by ordering
Gail Van Kleeck's
insightful, informational
books and CDs.**

E-BOOK

The Magical Interior Design Guide: Ideas for improving your inner spaces from the Home Decorating Fairy Godmother

If you have ever wished you could walk through your home with an interior designer who would give you budget respecting, easy to implement and confidence building information about making your surroundings more comfortable and welcoming, you will love ***The Magical Interior Design Guide***.

To order, go to:
www.homedecoratingfairygodmother.com

BOOKS

Make Your Move Magically Marvelous!

If you, or someone you know, is planning to move and feeling overwhelmed at the thought, you will be endlessly grateful for ***Make Your Move Magically Marvelous!***

This short and amazingly helpful little book is filled with suggestions and information about where to begin, sorting your belongings, creating storage, packing with unpacking in mind and preparing for the day of your move.

To order, go to: http://gailvankleeck.org/makeyourmovemagic/

How You See Anything is How You See Everything

A collection of short, tenderly-woven stories about life's ordinary moments and how what we focus on determines what we see. ***How You See Anything is How You See Everything*** is an insightful and inspiring little book that is small enough to fit on a bedside table and large enough to change a life.

To order, go to:
http://gailvankleeck.org/howseeanything

There is a Story Teller in My Closet

A little boy discovers a kind and magical story teller in his closet. She tells him stories about imaginary people, but the boy suspects they are really about him. ***There is a Story Teller in My Closet*** is about love and possibility and changing the way we see. It is a wise, tender and thought-provoking story for children of all ages.

To order go to:
http://gailvankleeck.org/simplewisdom

Simple Wisdom for Challenging Times

More than just another book of someone else's thoughts, **Simple Wisdom for Challenging Times** combines a list of A-Z observations with questions that make it a powerful tool for self-exploration and personal growth.

Opening and reading just one page a day can make a noticeable and meaningful difference in the way you see and live your life.

To order go to:
http://gailvankleeck.org/simplewisdom

CDs

What We Focus on Is What We See

What We Focus on Is What We See is a collection of stories from Gail Van Kleeck's book as well as others that are new. The combination of Gail's stories and her calming voice will draw you in and expand your sense of what is possible.

If you listen to this CD while you drive, you are very likely to arrive at your destination feeling more positive and peaceful.

To order, go to:
http://gailvankleeck.org/whatwefocuson

Imagine Walking Through Your New Front Door

This CD about moving is a companion to *Make Your Move Magically Marvelous!* It explores the power of creating a vision for your new home and reinforces some of the book's important themes.

Listening to this CD will inspire you to make your move with a more confident and possibility filled spirit.

To order, go to:
http://gailvankleeck.org/imaginewalking

NOTIFICATION LIST

If you email Gail at gail@homedecoratingfairygodmother.com and ask to be put on her contact list, you will be notified when her new books and products become available.

Made in the USA
Charleston, SC
21 November 2015